PUBLISHED BY ENVIEW RESEARCH AND DEVELOPMENT LABS
ISBN-13: 978-1511809146
ISBN-10: 1511809140

Alex Pappachen James
School of Engineering, Nazarbayev University, Astana, 010000
Kazakhstan.
apj@ieee.org

Ordering Information: Quantity sales. Special discounts are available on quantity purchases by corporations, associations, and others. For details, contact the publisher at the address above.

First printing, March 2015

Contents

I   An Introductory Guide to Raspberry Pi

1   What is Raspberry Pi? 7

1.1   The Raspberry Pi   **7**

1.1.1   Raspberry Pi Model A 7
1.1.2   Raspberry Pi Model A+ 8
1.1.3   Raspberry Pi Model B 8
1.1.4   Raspberry Pi Model B+ 8
1.1.5   Raspberry Pi 2 Model B 9

2   Basic Electronics 11

2.1   Basic Electronic Components   **11**

2.1.1   Resistor 11
2.1.2   Capacitor 12
2.1.3   Diode 13
2.1.4   Transistor 15

2.1.5   Intergrated Circuit 15

2.1.6   Battery 15

3   Setting up a Raspberry Pi 17

3.1   Setting up a Raspberry Pi   **17**

3.2   Installation Steps (for Beginners)   **18**

3.3   Installation Steps (for Advanced Users)   **18**

3.3.1   Setting up the SD Card 18

3.3.2   Connecting all the Components 20

3.3.3   Configuring the Raspberry Pi 20

4   Writing Programs in Pi 23

4.1   Hello World   **23**

4.2   Fundamentals of Python   **25**

5   Using the GPIO Pins 31

5.1   Accessing the GPIO Pins   **32**

5.1.1   Accessing from Terminal 32

5.1.2   Manipulating the GPIO using Python 33

6   Simple Projects in Pi 35

6.1   LED Blink Project   **35**

6.2   PIR Motion sensor as an Input device   **37**

6.3   Traffic Light   **40**

6.4   Switch   **43**

6.5   Burglar Alarm   **48**

6.6   Obstacle Avoidance Robot   **50**

7   Safety Measures 63

8   Troubleshooting the Pi 65

9   DIY Project Ideas 67

An Introductory Guide to Raspberry Pi

1   **What is Raspberry Pi?** 7

1.1   The Raspberry Pi

2   **Basic Electronics** 11

2.1   Basic Electronic Components

3   **Setting up a Raspberry Pi** 17

3.1   Setting up a Raspberry Pi
3.2   Installation Steps (for Beginners)
3.3   Installation Steps (for Advanced Users)

4   **Writing Programs in Pi** 23

4.1   Hello World
4.2   Fundamentals of Python

5   **Using the GPIO Pins** 31

5.1   Accessing the GPIO Pins

6   **Simple Projects in Pi** 35

6.1   LED Blink Project
6.2   PIR Motion sensor as an Input device
6.3   Traffic Light
6.4   Switch
6.5   Burglar Alarm
6.6   Obstacle Avoidance Robot

7   **Safety Measures** 63

8   **Troubleshooting the Pi** 65

9   **DIY Project Ideas** 67

1. What is Raspberry Pi?

1.1 The Raspberry Pi

Raspberry Pi is a low cost single computer developed by Raspberry Pi foundation, a charity based on UK. The Raspberry Pi can be connected to a monitor or a television and can be operated using a USB mouse and keyboard. The dimension of the device is comparable to that of a credit card and requires low operating power. It comprises all the commonly available interfaces used in general purposes computers such as USB ports, audio ports, HDMI output port, ethernet ports, etc. In addition to these standard interfaces, a number of general purpose input/output(GPIO) ports are also available in this device. These GPIO pins can configured to act either as an input or as an output port, thereby making the device to function as a low power high performance embedded system. There are several versions of the Raspberry Pi available in market depending on the features provided. A brief history regarding the development of this board is given in the following sections.

1.1.1 Raspberry Pi Model A

The Raspberry Pi model A was the very first Raspberry Pi device introduced by the Raspberry Pi foundation. It has a dimension of 85.6mm x 56.5mm. It comprises of a 700MHz single cored ARM 11 processor with 256 MB of RAM and a single USB port. It has no ethernet port for internet connectivity and possesses a number of 17 GPIO pins. The

Figure 1.1: The Raspberry Pi (Model B+)

HDMI port present in the device allows it to be connected to a compatible monitor/television. A secure digital(SD) card is used for installing the OS as well as for storage purposes.

1.1.2   Raspberry Pi Model A+

The Raspberry Pi model A+ has similar features as that of the model A, except for the increased number of GPIO pins as well as the change in the storage card used. It has 9 GPIO pins in addition to the 17 pins found in the model A, thereby making a total of 26 GPIO pins. For storage purposes, the SD card found in model A was replaced with a micro-SD card. The dimension also got reduced to 65mm x 56.5mm.

1.1.3   Raspberry Pi Model B

In the Raspberry Pi Model B, the RAM is increased to 512MB compared to the 256MB present in the previous versions. Also, an additional USB port was introduced along with an ethernet port for connecting to the internet. All other features were same as that of the previous two models. The dimension of the device was same as that of the model A. The number of GPIO pins is 17. The model B also used SD card as its storage device.

1.1.4   Raspberry Pi Model B+

The major differences between the model B+ and its previous version, the model B are the addition of USB ports and GPIO pins. The model B+ has four USB ports and 26 GPIO pins. It also used a micro-SD card instead of the SD card found in model B.

1.1.5 Raspberry Pi 2 Model B

The Raspberry Pi 2 model B, which is considered to be the second generation of the Raspberry Pi devices is the first device to undergo a major upgradation since the introduction of the original board in 2012. It has a powerful 900MHz quad core ARM cortex A7 processor along with 1GB of RAM. All other features are same as that of the model B+ with four USB ports, HDMI output port, 2.5mm audio output port, ethernet port and micro-SD based storage.

2. Basic Electronics

2.1   Basic Electronic Components

Raspberry Pi is not just a computer. With Raspberry Pi, we have options to connect electronic components which enables us to understand and manipulate real-world entities. Raspberry Pi allows us to connect electronic devices or components through its GPIO pins. The chapter gives an introduction to few basic electronic components/devices before we use them in real electronic projects.

2.1.1   Resistor

Resistor is a device used to control the current flowing through an electronic circuit. Resistors(2.1) offer a resistance to the flow of electric current and thereby acts as a current controller. Resistors are not polarity sensitive devices which means they can be connected in either direction as there is no positive and negative terminals for a resistor.

Resistor value is defined in terms of Ohms(Ω). As the value of resistor in ohms increases higher will be the resistance offered by the device against the flow of current in the circuit. Resistors are of different types.

i) Variable resistor: These resistors has a control attached to it that allows the user to change the resistance value. These are also known as potentiometers.

ii) Voltage dependent resistor: These can change the resistance value according to the

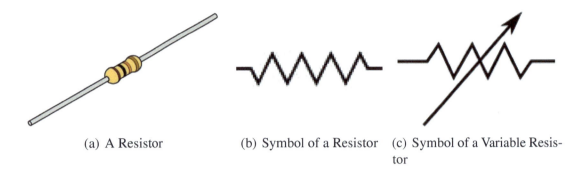

(a) A Resistor   (b) Symbol of a Resistor   (c) Symbol of a Variable Resistor

Figure 2.1: The Resistor

voltage applied across it.

iii) Temperature dependent resistor: Such resistors are capable of changing their resistance value depending on the ambient temperature. Based on whether the resistance is increasing or decreasing when the temperature is increased, two types of temperature dependent resistors exists: positive temperature coefficient and negative temperature coefficient resistors. The positive temperature coefficient resistors will increase their resistance value on increasing the temperature while the negative temperature coefficient resistor will decrease its resistance value when the temperature is increased. These are also called as thermistors.

iv) Light dependent resistor(LDR): LDRs are special type of resistors that can change their resistance value depending on the amount of light falling over it. These are used to detect the presence of ambient light.

The resistance value of a resistor is written over its body using a set of coloured rings. The colour code used to define the resistance value of a resistor is given below:

There will be four colored rings (see Fig.2.2) present in the body of the resistor. The first two rings indicate the first two digits of the resistance the value. The third ring indicates the multiplier value, represented as a power of 10. The fourth ring gives the tolerance of the resistor, which is a parameter used to depict how close the actual value of the resistor is to the value mentioned on the resistor. In Fig.2.2, the first two rings are red coloured which tells us that the first two digits of the resistance value is 22. The third ring is black in colour. Therefore, the multiplier is 100. The fourth ring is golden coloured indicating a tolerance of ±5%. Thus the resistor value of the resistance shown is 22Ω with a tolerance of ±5%.

2.1.2 Capacitor

Capacitors are devices that are used to store electric charges temporarily. The capacitance of a capacitor is measured in terms of microFarad(μF). Similar to variable resistors, variable capacitors are also present. Unlike resistors, some type of capacitors are polarity sensitive.

Colour	Digit	Multiplier	Tolerance(%)
Black	0	$10^0 = 1$	-
Brown	1	10^1	1
Red	2	10^2	2
Orange	3	10^3	-
Yellow	4	10^4	-
Green	5	10^5	.5
Blue	6	10^6	.25
Violet	7	10^7	.1
Grey	8	10^8	-
White	9	10^9	-
Gold	-	10^{-1}	5
Silver	-	10^{-2}	10
None	-	-	20

Table 2.1: Resistor color codes

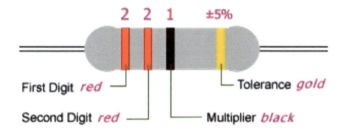

Figure 2.2: Color coding on a resistor

Therefore, one should be careful while connecting a capacitor to a circuit. The negative polarity terminal of the capacitor should be connected to the negative terminal of the battery and the positive terminal of the capacitor should be connected to the positive terminal of the battery.

2.1.3 Diode

Diode is one of the commonly used semiconductor devices in electronic circuits. Diode (Fig.2.4) is a uni-directional device. That is, it can transmit current in one direction only. It will not allow current to flow through it from the other direction. Because of this property of diodes, they are used in circuits to facilitate the flow of current only in one direction. Current always flow from Anode to Cathode terminal of the diode. i.e., in a circuit, current

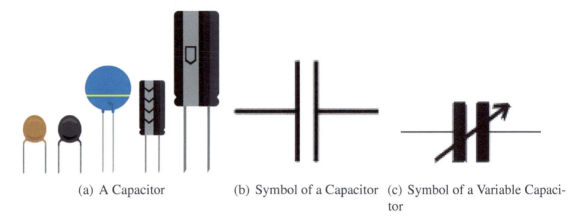

(a) A Capacitor   (b) Symbol of a Capacitor   (c) Symbol of a Variable Capacitor

Figure 2.3: The Capacitor

(a) A Diode   (b) Symbol of a Diode

Figure 2.4: The Diode

will flow only if the positive terminal of the battery is connected to the anode and the negative terminal of battery to the cathode. Current will not flow through the circuit if the connections are reversed.

Light emitting diodes(LEDs) are a special type of diodes that are capable of producing light when current flows through it. They will emit a light only if the anode of the LED is connected to the positive terminal of battery and the cathode is connected to negative terminal.

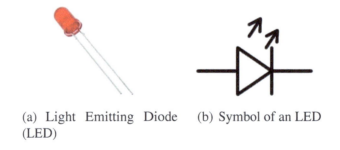

(a) Light Emitting Diode   (b) Symbol of an LED
(LED)

Figure 2.5: Light Emitting Diode

2.1.4 Transistor

Transistors are semiconductor devices with three terminals called base(B), emitter(E) and collector(C). Transistors are capable of controlling the current that flows across its emitter and collector terminals by varying the voltage applied to the base terminal. They are commonly used in amplifier circuits.

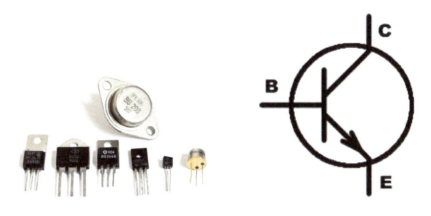

(a) Different types of transistors   (b) Symbol of a transistor

Figure 2.6: Transistor

2.1.5 Intergrated Circuit

Integrated circuits(ICs) are small devices that contain an entire circuit. A typical IC may contain almost all the basic components that we have seen till now such as resistors, capacitors, diodes, transistors, etc.

2.1.6 Battery

A battery is a source of electrical energy that can be used to power up electronic devices. These devices contain chemicals that can undergo chemical reactions to produce electrical energy. Batteries have two terminals- positive and negative terminals. A battery is described in terms of its voltage, current and capacity. The voltage rating indicates the maximum voltage that it is capable of providing when in fully charged condition. The current rating is the maximum current the battery can output to the circuit. The voltage and current ratings are mentioned in terms of Volt(V) and Ampere(A) respectively. The battery capacity is specified in terms of Ampere-hour(Ah). This gives the time taken for a battery to discharge from fully charged state to its cut off state when a constant current is drawn from it continuously.

3. Setting up a Raspberry Pi

3.1 Setting up a Raspberry Pi

The first thing that we do after buying a new computer is to install an operating system followed by all the necessary softwares. As mentioned above, the Raspberry Pi is a single board computer and it requires an operating system for it to function. The only operating system supported by the Raspberry Pi upto model B+ versions is Linux OS. The latest version of the board, Raspberry Pi 2 B also supports Android and windows operating systems. The OS is installed on the SD/micro-SD card used with the device. All Linux distributions cannot be used with Raspberry Pi since the architecture is different than the general purpose computers. The OS compatible with Raspberry Pi is also provided by the Raspberry foundation itself. You have two options for installing the OS. The first options is for beginners and the second option is for advanced users. We will discuss both these methods in detail below. The items required for the installation are as below:

1. Raspberry Pi B+
2. 8GB SD card or microSD card with adaptor
3. SD Card reader or microSD card reader
4. HDMI/DVI/VGA compatible monitor/television
5. HDMI cable or HDMI to DVI/VGA convertor
6. USB Mouse

7. USB Keyboard
8. Micro-USB to USB cable or a micro-USB power cable

3.2 Installation Steps (for Beginners)

This installation process is called new out of the box software(NOOBS) setup. Users can either buy a NOOBS SD card from online stores or they can download NOOBS from the website

`http://www.raspberrypi.org/downloads/`

If you are downloading the NOOBS from the website, then follow the steps given here.

1. Download the NOOBS file from the above mentioned website.
2. Extract the contents of the zip file.
3. Copy the extracted files to the SD card
4. Now we have the NOOBS SD card

Once the NOOBS SD card is ready, the installation process is as shown below

1. Insert the SD card to the Raspberry Pi
2. Connect the keyboard, mouse and the monitor
3. Power up the device using a micro-USB power adaptor or a micro-USB cable connected to a computer/laptop
4. The device will boot and a window will come up listing the operating systems that can be installed. Select Raspbian from the list and click the Install button
5. The device will start the installation process which will take some time to finish
6. Once the installation process is completed, the raspi-config menu will be open.
7. Select Finish from the menu and press enter
8. The device will reboot and a prompt asking for the username will appear. The default username is pi. Type in this and press enter. Now the prompt will ask for the password which is raspberry. After entering the password, type in startx to invoke the GUI

3.3 Installation Steps (for Advanced Users)

Advanced users can download the Raspbian image file from the Raspberry Pi download website and set it up to the SD directly which is time saving compared to the NOOBS setup process. The installation process can be summarised in the following steps:

3.3.1 Setting up the SD Card

First, download the latest version of the **Raspbian** OS, which is an OS distribution provided by the manufacturer of the device. It can be obtained from

`http://www.raspberrypi.org/downloads/`

Extract the zip file downloaded to a folder of your choice. After that, download another software called **Win32DiskImager** from the website
`http://sourceforge.net/projects/win32diskimager/files/latest/download`
Install the software. Win32DiskImager is a software used for writing operating system image files to USB devices and SD cards. After that, insert you SD card to the card reader. Then, right click on the Win32DiskImager.exe file and select **Run as administrator** option. Select the SD card from the drop down menu (shown in Fig.3.1) located at the right side.

Figure 3.1: Selecting the Target USB Device

Click on the icon located before the drive selection drop down menu (shown in Fig.3.2) for selecting the operating system image.

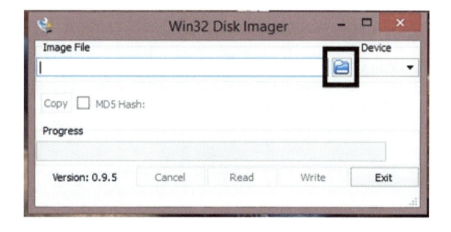

Figure 3.2: Select an Operating System Image

Select the OS image that you have extracted before using the window that just opened.

The write option at the bottom will become active now. Click on this button to start copying the OS to the SD card. Once the entire operation is completed, remove your SD card. Now your SD card contains a bootable operating system.

3.3.2 Connecting all the Components

Connect all the necessary hardwares to your Raspberry Pi. This include the HDMI cable for the display, mouse, and the keyboard. Then, insert the SD card that contains the operating system. After that, connect the micro-USB power cable. A smartphone power adaptor or a micro-USB cable connected to a computer or laptop can be used for powering the device. Once the device is powered, it will switch ON by itself and the booting process can be seen on the display connected.

3.3.3 Configuring the Raspberry Pi

Some configuration settings have to be altered when the Raspberry Pi is booted for the first time. Once the device completes the booting up process, a **raspi-config** window will open that lists the various settings available for the user to change. After installing the OS, the SD card will use up only the storage space it requires. The remaining memory won't be available for the user for installing other applications. So, the first thing one has to do after installing the OS for the first time is to free up the remaining memory. For this, follow the steps given below:

a) Select the **expand_rootfs** option from the menu (shown in Fig.3.3) and press the Enter button

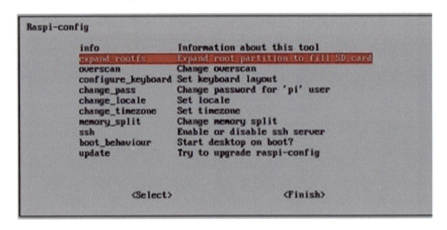

Figure 3.3: The Raspi-config screen

b) Confirm that you want to expand the file system from the message that is shown

c) After a few moments, you will get back to the configuration list. Then select the finish option that is given in the bottom of the list

d) Confirm that you want to reboot the system

The Raspberry Pi will then reboot by itself. It will take some time to complete the booting process since the expansion of file system is being done. Once it finishes the booting process, you will see a login prompting you enter the username. The default username and password of the Raspbian OS are:

username: pi

password: raspberry

If there is no error in the username and password that you have typed, you would be logged in by now.

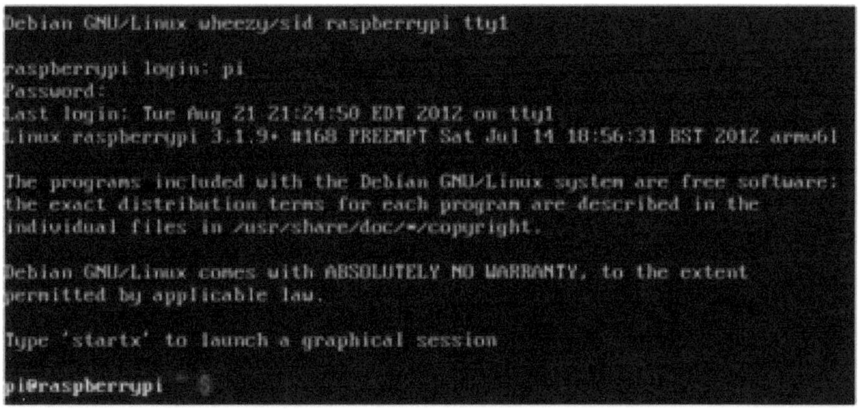

Figure 3.4: After a successful login

Type startx at the prompt and press the Enter key. It will start the GUI environment of the OS.

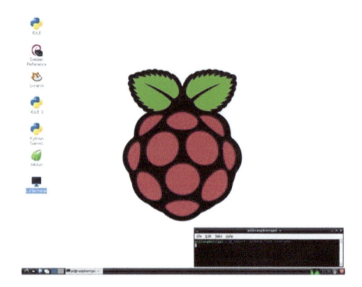

Figure 3.5: The Graphical User Interface (Rasbian OS)

```
otwrite(ast):
odename = getNodename()
label=symbol.sym_name.get(int(ast[0]), ast..
        %s [label="%s' % (nodename, label),
print
if isinstance(ast[1], str):
    if ast[1].strip():
        print   = %s"] ;   % ast[1]
    else:
        print '"]'

else:
    print '"]'
    children = []
    for n, child in enumerate(ast[1:]):
        children.append(dotwrite(child))
    print          %s -> {  % nodename,
    for name in children:
        print '%s  % name,
```

4. Writing Programs in Pi

4.1   Hello World

Raspberry Pi comes preloaded with Python compiler. The following example will explain
how to write a simple program to display a message using python in Raspberry Pi. Open
IDLE3 by double clicking on the icon in the desktop. IDLE3 is an interactive development
environment(IDE) for python.

Figure 4.1: Python Command Interpreter

Click on **File–>New Window**. It will open up a new window, where you write your program. Type the following program into the new window:

```
print('Hello there!')\\
username = input("Enter your name ")\\
print ('Nice to meet you, ' + username + '.  Have a nice day!')
```

Click on **File–>Save As**. In the dialog box that opens up, enter a file name for your program and click save. After that, select **Run–>Run Module** or press the **F5** button on the keyboard. This will execute the program. In the **IDLE3** window, you will get a prompt stating "Enter your name". Type in your name and press the enter key. You will see the output.

Figure 4.2: Example output

4.2 Fundamentals of Python

In this section, we introduce the fundamentals of programming in Python and learn the basic constructs required to start programming in python. Python is an open source scripting language developed by Guido van Rossum in the early 1990s.

Basic Datatypes

Integers: This is the default datatype for numbers.

```
z=4
z=5/2
```

Floats

```
x=3.125
```

Strings: We can use "" or '' to specify strings. That is both "abc" and 'abc' are same. We can use triple double quotes (""" """) for multi-line strings or strings that contain both ' and " inside. """a'b"c"""

Assignment

It should be noted that binding a variable in Python means setting a name to hold a reference to some object.

- Assignment creates references, not copies.
- Names in Python do not have an intrinsic type. Objects have types.
- Python determines the type of the reference automatically based on the data object assigned to it.
- You create a name the first time it appears on the left side of an assignment expression: x = 3
- A reference is deleted via garbage collection after any names bound to it have passed out of scope.

Naming Rules

Names are case sensitive and cannot start with a number. They can contain letters, numbers, and underscores.

```
bob   Bob   _bob   _2_bob_   bob_2   BoB
```

There are some reserved words:

```
and,  assert,  break,  class,  continue,  def,  del,
elif,  else,  except,  exec,  finally,  for,  from,
global,  if,  import,  in,  is,  lambda,  not,  or,
pass,  print,  raise,  return,  try,  while
```

Sequence Types: Tuples, Lists and Strings

In addition to the basic datatypes in python, you can use sequences for storing, organizing and manipulating more complex data. Here we take a quick glance on sequences.

1. Tuple
- A simple immutable ordered sequence of items
- Items can be of mixed types, including collection types.
- Tuples are defined using parentheses (and commas).

```
>>> tu = (23,'abc', 4.56, (2,3), 'def')
```

2. Strings
- Immutable
- Conceptually very much like a tuple

```
>>> st  =  "Hello  World"
>>> st  =  'Hello  World'
>>> st  =  """This  is  a  multi-line
string  that  uses  triple  quotes."""
```

3. List
- Mutable ordered sequence of items of mixed types

```
>>> li  =  ["abc", 34, 4.34, 23]
```

All the three sequence types (tuples, strings ans lists) share much of the same syntax and functionality. The key difference is that tuples and strings are immutable, but lists are mutable.

We can access invidual members of a tuple, list or string using square bracket "array" notation. Note that the indexing of all the tuple, list and string starts with 0.

```
>>> tu =(23, 'abc', 4.56, (2,3), 'def')
>>> tu[1]          #Second item in the tuple
        'abc'

>>> li =["abc", 34, 4.34, 23]
>>> li[1]          #Second item in the list
        34

>>> st ="Hello  World"
>>> st[1]          #Second item in the string
        'e'
```

The "in" Operator

The operator "in" enables us to perform a boolean test to check whether a value is inside a container or not.

```
>>> t =[1, 2, 4, 5]
>>> 3 in t
False
>>> 4 in t
True
>>> 4 not in t
False
```

In the case of strings, we can use the "in" operator for testing the presence of a substring

```
>>> a='abcde'
>>> 'c' in a
True
>>> 'cd' in a
True
>>> 'ac' in a
False
```

The "+" operator

The "+" is used to generate a new tuple, list or string from an existing one.

```
>>> (1,2,3)+(4,5,6)
(1,2,3,4,5,6)

>>> [1,2,3]+[4,5,6]
[1,2,3,4,5,6]

>>> "Hello"+" "+"World"
'Hello World'
```

The "*" operator

The "*" operator produces a new tuple, list or string that "repeats" the original content.

```
>>> (1,2,3)*3
(1,2,3,1,2,3,1,2,3)

>>> [1,2,3]*3
[1,2,3,1,2,3,1,2,3]

>>> "Hello"*3
'HelloHelloHello'
```

Functions in Python

Programming languages, in general supports the use of functions. The functions enables a programmer to manage complexity by writing different tasks as different callable modules which can be integrated later.

Following is an example definition of a function

```
def get_final_answer(filename):
        "Documentation String"
        line1
        line2
        return total_counter
```

You can see the following in the above function definition
- A function definition always begin with "def"
- "get_final_answer" is the name of the function defined above.
- "filename" is the argument(like an input) of the function.
- We should give a ":"(colon) after the "def" statement
- The indentation matters. First line with less indentation is considered to be outside of the function definition.
- The keyword "return" indicates the value to be sent back to the caller.

Calling a Function

The syntax for a function call is

```
>>> def myfun(x,y):
                return x*y
>>> myfun(3,4)
12
```

Logical Expressions

True and False

True and False are constants in python. Comparison operators in python include ==,!=, <, <= etc.

X==Y : Checks whether X and Y has the same value.

X!=Y : Checks whether X is not equal to Y.

You can also combine Boolean expressions
- **true** if a is true and b is true: **a and b**
- **true** if a is true or b is true: **a or b**
- **true** if a is false: **not a**

Control Flow

There are several Python expressions that control the flow of a program. All of them make use of Boolean conditional tests.

- **if** Statements.
- **while** Loops.
- **assert** Statements.
- **for** Loops.

1. If Statement:

```
if x==3:
        print "X equals 3."
elif x==2:
        print "X equals 2."
else:
        print "X equals something else"
print "This is outside the if statement"
```

2. while Loops:

```
x=3
while x<10:
        x=x+1
        print "Still in the loop"
print "Outside of the loop"
```

3. assert:

An **assert** statement will check to make sure that something is tue during the course of a program. If the condition is false, the program stops.

```
assert(number_of_players <5)
```

3. For Loops:

A for loop steps through each of the items in a list, tuple, string or any other type of object which is "iterable"

```
for <item> in <collection >:
        <statements >
```

If <collection> is a list or a tuple, then the loop steps through each element of the sequence. If <collection> is a string , then the loop steps through each character of the string.

```
for someChar in "Hello World":
        print someChar
```

5. Using the GPIO Pins

Apart from the USB ports, HDMI port, and the 3.5mm audio out port, the Raspberry Pi also possesses some other ports which can be used either as an input port or as an output port. Such types of ports that can act both as input as well as an output are present in all the embedded systems and are called general purpose input output(GPIO) ports. We can change the behaviour of these ports via programming. The GPIO ports in Raspberry Pi support digital output and input only. If a GPIO pin is set as an input port, and a voltage greater than 2V is applied, the input is considered as a digital high by the device and vice versa. When the GPIO pin is configured as an output port and if we write a digital low to the port, an output voltage less than 0.5V will be outputted through the port. On the other hand, when a digital high is send to the port, a voltage greater than 2.5V and less than 3.3V will be outputted.

The GPIO pins are arranged in two rows near the RCA video out port(yellow connector). It should also be noted that all the pins are not GPIO pins. These include power pins that can output a voltage of 3.3V or 5V as well as ground pins. The GPIO pins of the Raspberry Pi module can be invoked in two ways, namely, the BOARD mode and the BCM mode. In the BOARD mode, the pins are named by counting the pins across and down from pin1. For example, the fourth pin present in the board will be referred to as 4 itself while programming. On the other method, there is a number pre-assigned to each GPIO pin. This number should be used for changing the behaviour of a particular GPIO pin. For example, the 11th pin in the board is assigned as GPIO17 in BCM mode. So one has to remember the GPIO names of each pins while using the BCM mode. The BCM mode based pin diagram of the Raspberry Pi devices is shown in following figure.

Figure 5.1: GPIO Pins (Model B+ and Pi 2 B)

5.1   Accessing the GPIO Pins

The GPIO pins can be accessed directly from the terminal as well as from a programming language. In this section, we will see how this can be done from the terminal window and using python language.

5.1.1   Accessing from Terminal

This is done by creating a file in the **/sys/class/gpio/export** subdirectory. The procedure is as follows:

a. Type in **sudo echo 11 > /sys/class/gpio/export**

This will create a GPIO structure that is capable of controlling the GPIO11 of the Raspberry Pi. By changing 11, the required GPIO pin can be accessed.

b. Type in **sudo echo out > /sys/class/gpio/gpio11/direction**

This will configure the GPIO to act as an output port. For configuring to be an input, replace in with out.

c. Enter **sudo echo 1 > /sys/class/gpio/gpio11/value**

This command is used to output a logic high(1) to the GPIO11. Logic low can be out by replacing 1 with 0.

5.1.2 Manipulating the GPIO using Python

In python, before using the GPIO, a suitable library must be installed. The newer versions of Raspbian OS has this library pre-installed. To install the GPIO library, open terminal and type in the following command

sudo apt-get install rpi.gpio

This will install the latest version of the library. If the library is already installed, then it will be upgraded to the latest version, if available.

Sample Python program using board mode:

```
import RPi.GPIO as GPIO #import the GPIO library
GPIO.setmode(GPIO.BOARD) #Select board mode
GPIO.setup(11, GPIO.IN)  #11th pin as input
GPIO.setup(12, GPIO.OUT) #12th pin as output
input_value = GPIO.input(11) # Read value from 11th pin
GPIO.output(12, GPIO.HIGH) #Output logic 1 to 12th pin
```

Sample Python program using BCM mode:

```
import RPi.GPIO as GPIO #import the GPIO library
GPIO.setmode(GPIO.BCM) # Select BCM mode
GPIO.setup(17, GPIO.IN) )  #GPIO17 as input
GPIO.setup(18, GPIO.OUT) #GPIO18 as output
input_value = GPIO.input(17) # Read value from GPIO17
GPIO.output(18, GPIO.HIGH) #Output logic 1 to GPIO18
```

The GPIO.BOARD option indicates that you are referring to the pins according to the order of pin number in the raspberry pi board. The GPIO.BOARD refers to those pins shown in the middle of Fig.5.1. On the other hand, GPIO.BCM refers to the pins by the "Broadcom SOC Channel" number. These numbers are indicated as green rectangles in Fig.5.1. The problem with the BCM based numbering is that the numbering varies across different versions of the model B of Raspberry Pi and you will need to figure out the right numbers when you shift between boards. However, it is safer to use the BOARD based numbering in your programs if you are planning to use more than one type of Pi in a single project.

6. Simple Projects in Pi

6.1 LED Blink Project

In this section, we discuss a simple project that enables us to control an LED using the Raspberry Pi (Model B+). In addition to the Raspberry Pi, we would require the following components:

1. **Breadboard**
2. **LED**
3. **Resistor (180Ω)**
4. **Jumper wires(Male to Female).**

We are trying to create an LED blinking project on a breadboard with the help of Raspberry Pi. We are using a breadboard to avoid soldering tasks. Make connections as shown in Fig. 6.1

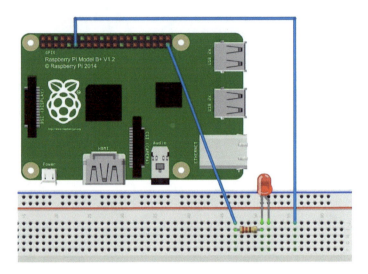

Figure 6.1: LED Blink (Schematic Diagram)

Here we use a resitor in the cicuit for limiting the current flowing through the LED. It is important to note that the longer lead of the LED is the anode(+) and the shorter one is the cathode(-). In Fig. 6.1, **GPIO17** of the Pi board is connected to the anode of the LED and the cathode lead of the LED has a connection to one end of the resistor and the other end of the resistor is connected to the ground(**GND**) pin of the Pi board.

Now we are ready to write a program in python to control the LED connected to **GPIO17** of the board. The following python program when run gives an LED blinking effect.

```
import RPi.GPIO as GPIO
import time

GPIO.setmode(GPIO.BOARD)
GPIO.setup(11,GPIO.OUT)

while True:
    GPIO.output(11,True)
    time.sleep(1)            #One second delay
    GPIO.output(11,False)
    time.sleep(1)            #One second delay
```

The statement

```
import RPi.GPIO as GPIO
```

is used to import the library which allow us to logically access the GPIO pins of the board.

```
import time
```

is used to import the time library for accessing the sleep function.

```
GPIO.setmode(GPIO.BOARD)
```

indicates that we are using the BOARD numbering scheme discussed earlier.

```
GPIO.setup(11,GPIO.OUT)
```

sets pin number 11 to act as an ouput pin.

Inside the while loop, we have statements to turn the LED ON and OFF. It is important to use the sleep functions in between those statements in order for us to see the blinking. If we do not use a sleep statement, then we will not be able to see any blinking because of the higher switching speeds.

Keeping all the circuit connections intact, the BCM version of the same program will look like the following

```
import RPi.GPIO as GPIO
import time

GPIO.setmode(GPIO.BCM)
GPIO.setup(17,GPIO.OUT)

while True:
    GPIO.output(17,True)
    time.sleep(1)              #One second delay
    GPIO.output(17,False)
    time.sleep(1)              #One second delay
```

6.2 PIR Motion sensor as an Input device

A Passive InfraRed sensor (PIR sensor) is an electronic sensing device that allows us to sense motion (especially, whether a human has moved in or out of the sensors range) by measuring the InfraRed (IR) light radiating from objects in its field of view. They are most often used in PIR-based motion detectors. The PIR takes the output of a pyroelectic sensor and does some minor processing on it with the help of the bunch of supporting circuitry along with some resistors and capacitors, to emit a digital output pulse from the analog sensor.

Figure 6.2: PIR motion sensor

The PIR motion sensors are small, inexpensive, low-power, easy to use and they don't wear out. Hence they are commonly found in appliances and gadgets used in homes or businesses. They are often referred to as PIR, "Passive InfraRed", "Pyroelectric", or "IR motion" sensors.

Figure 6.2 shows the PIR sensor and Figure 6.3 shows its corresponding connection header pins. The program for the circuit diagram shown in Figure 6.4 is given below. The connections has been summarized in the Table 6.1.

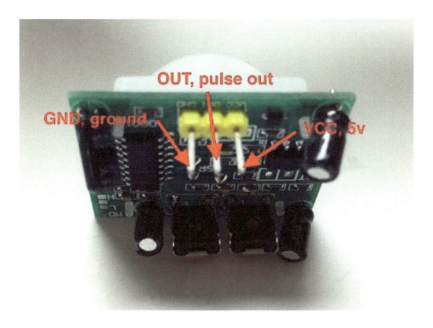

Figure 6.3: PIR motion sensor Pins

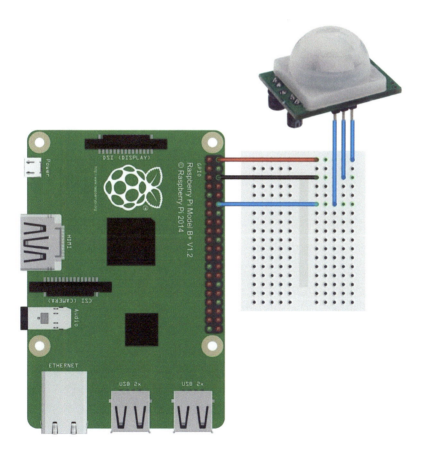

Figure 6.4: Circuit Diagram

Raspberry Pi Board	PIR motion sensor
2 (Vcc)	Vcc
6 (Gnd)	Gnd
12 (I/O pin	Vout(Digital signal output)

Table 6.1: Circuit Connection

Program

```
import RPi.GPIO as GPIO
import time
GPIO.setmode(GPIO.BOARD)
GPIO.setwarnings(False)
'''Configuring the pin 12 of Raspberry Pi board as input for
receiving the PIR digital pin output'''
GPIO.setup(12,GPIO.IN)

while True:
        in_st = GPIO.input(12)
        print('Status : ',in_st)
        if in_st == True:
#Output message on detecting a movement in the range of PIR
motion sensor
                print('Motion Detected')
                time.sleep(1)
```

6.3 Traffic Light

Traffic lights are signalling devices positioned at road intersections, pedestrian crossings and other locations to control competing flows of traffic. Traffic lights alternate the right of way accorded to road users by displaying lights of a standard color (red, yellow, and green) following a universal color code as described in Table 6.2.

Figure 6.5 shows the Traffic Light System that utilizes LED technology. The controlling of the traffic light sequence can be acheived using the Raspberry Pi GPIO pins. A typical example design with the specification shown in Table 6.3 is discussed here in detail using simple LEDs. The program for the circuit diagram shown in Figure 6.6 is given below. The

Traffic Control Signal	Purpose
Red	The color 'red' on the signal light indicates to stop well before the stop line and not to crowd the intersection. Turn left in a red signal only when there is a sign to do so. While turning, yield the right of way to pedestrians and vehicles coming from other directions.
Amber (Yellow)	The amber (or yellow) light indicates to clear the road when the signal is changing from green to red. If, by mistake, caught in the amber signal in the middle of a large road crossing, continue with care and do not accelerate in panic.
Green	The signal light 'green' set you to go but be careful while on the start of move. Check whether vehicles from other directions have cleared the road. Suppose you want to turn left or right, check the signal whether it allows or not separately. If yes, turn but yield the right of way to pedestrians and vehicles from other directions.

Table 6.2: Traffic Control Light Standard (India)

connections has been summarized in the Table 6.4.

Program

```
import RPi.GPIO as GPIO
import time

GPIO.setmode(GPIO.BOARD)
GPIO.setwarnings(False)
GPIO.setup(12,GPIO.OUT) # Red Light
```

Figure 6.5: Traffic Light

```
GPIO.setup(16,GPIO.OUT) # Yellow Light
GPIO.setup(18,GPIO.OUT) # Green Light

def setinitialize:
        GPIO.output(12,False)
        GPIO.output(16,False)
        GPIO.output(18,False)
        count = 0; # For initialization purposes only.

while True:
        if count == 0:
                setinitialize();
        count = 1;
        GPIO.output(12,True)
        GPIO.output(16,False)
```

Traffic Control Signal	Duration (minutes)
Red	3
Amber (Yellow)	0.5
Green	3

Table 6.3: Design Specification for the Traffic Light Example

Raspberry Pi Board	LED
6 (Gnd)	short legs (-ve terminal) of Red, Yellow & Green LEDs
12 (I/O pin)	long leg (+ve terminal) of Red LED
16 (I/O pin)	long leg (+ve terminal) of Yellow LED
18 (I/O pin)	long leg (+ve terminal) of Green LED

Table 6.4: Circuit Connection

```
        GPIO.output(18,False)
#3 minutes (60 x 3 = 180 seconds) delay
        time.sleep(180)

        GPIO.output(12,False)
        GPIO.output(16,True)
        GPIO.output(18,False)
#0.5 minutes (60 x 0.5 = 30 seconds) delay
        time.sleep(30)

        GPIO.output(12,False)
        GPIO.output(16,False)
        GPIO.output(18,True)
#3 minutes (60 x 3 = 180 seconds) delay
        time.sleep(3)
```

6.4 Switch

A push-button (also spelled pushbutton) or simply button is a simple switch mechanism for controlling some aspect of a machine or a process. Buttons are typically made out of hard material, usually plastic or metal.[1] The surface is usually flat or shaped to accommodate the human finger or hand, so as to be easily depressed or pushed. Buttons are most often biased switches, though even many un-biased buttons (due to their physical nature) require a spring to return to their un-pushed state.

Uses

The "push-button" has been utilized in calculators, push-button telephones, kitchen appliances, and various other mechanical and electronic devices, home and commercial.

In industrial and commercial applications, push buttons can be connected together by a mechanical linkage so that the act of pushing one button causes the other button to be released. In this way, a stop button can "force" a start button to be released. This method of linkage is used in simple manual operations in which the machine or process have no electrical circuits for control.

Pushbuttons are often color-coded to associate them with their function so that the operator will not push the wrong button in error. Commonly used colors are red for stopping the machine or process and green for starting the machine or process.

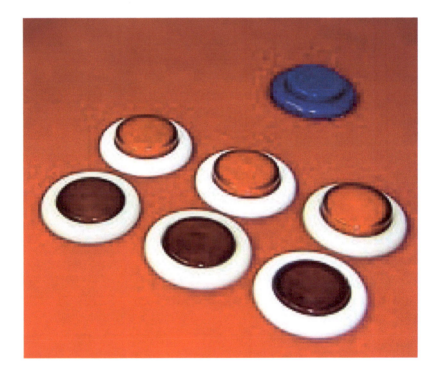

Figure 6.9: Generic arcade game buttons

Red pushbuttons can also have large heads (called mushroom heads) for easy operation and to facilitate the stopping of a machine. These pushbuttons are called emergency stop buttons and are mandated by the electrical code in many jurisdictions for increased safety.

This large mushroom shape can also be found in buttons for use with operators who need to wear gloves for their work and could not actuate a regular flush-mounted push button. As an aid for operators and users in industrial or commercial applications, a pilot light is commonly added to draw the attention of the user and to provide feedback if the button is pushed. Typically this light is included into the center of the pushbutton and a lens replaces the pushbutton hard center disk. The source of the energy to illuminate the light is not directly tied to the contacts on the back of the pushbutton but to the action the pushbutton controls. In this way a start button when pushed will cause the process or machine operation to be started and a secondary contact designed into the operation or process will close to turn on the pilot light and signify the action of pushing the button caused the resultant process or action to start.

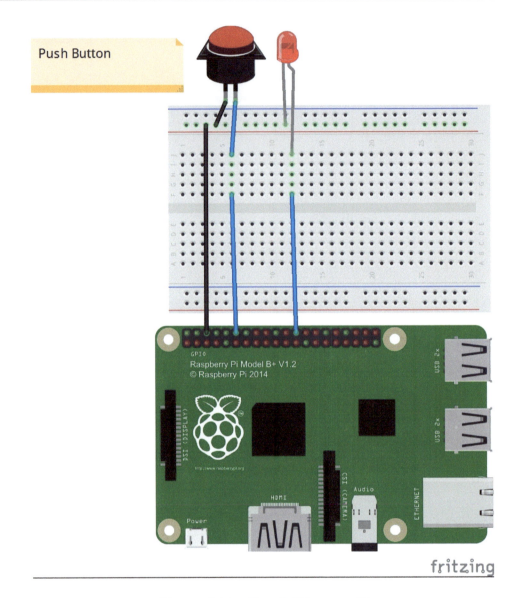

Figure 6.11: Circuit Diagram II

Raspberry Pi Board	Switch
6 (Gnd)	short leg (-ve terminal) of Push-button switch
12 (I/O pin)	long leg (+ve terminal) of Push-button switch

Table 6.5: Circuit Connection I

Raspberry Pi Board	Components
6 (Gnd)	short leg (-ve terminal) of Push-button switch & Red LED
12 (I/O pin)	long leg (+ve terminal) of Push-button switch
24 (I/O pin)	long leg (+ve terminal) of Red LED

Table 6.6: Circuit Connection II

Program

a) Program for Circuit Connection shown in Figure 6.10

```
import RPi.GPIO as GPIO
import time

GPIO.setmode(GPIO.BOARD)
GPIO.setwarnings(False)
#connect one leg to GND
GPIO.setup(11,GPIO.IN,pull_up_down=GPIO.PUD_UP)
while True:
        ButtonPress1 = GPIO.input(11)

        if ButtonPress1 == False:
                print('Button Status:',ButtonPress1)
                time.sleep(0.1)
```

b) Program for Circuit Connection shown in Figure 6.11

```
import RPi.GPIO as GPIO
import time

GPIO.setmode(GPIO.BOARD)
GPIO.setwarnings(False)
GPIO.setup(11,GPIO.IN,pull_up_down=GPIO.PUD_UP)

GPIO.setup(12,GPIO.OUT)
led_status = False

while True:
        ButtonPress1 = GPIO.input(11)
```

```
if ButtonPress1 == False:
        led_status = not led_status
        GPIO.output(12,led_status)
        print('led status ',led_status)
        time.sleep(0.1)
else:

        GPIO.output(12,led_status)
        print('Button Press not Detected',
        ButtonPress1)
```

6.5 Burglar Alarm

Burglar Alarm is an alarm used for security purposes. The security alarm can be defined as a system designed to detect intrusion – unauthorized entry – into a building or area. Security alarms are used in residential, commercial, industrial, and military properties for protection against burglary (theft) or property damage, as well as personal protection against intruders. Car alarms likewise protect vehicles and their contents. Prisons also use security systems for control of inmates. Here, we consider the design of a system with PIR motion sensor and Buzzer controlled remotely by a Raspberry Pi module.

In general terms, a buzzer may be understood as a device that can produce an audible tone in the influence of an externally applied voltage. This audible output may be either in the form of a buzzing or a beeping sound. The sound is created by inducing rapid movements in the diaphragm of the buzzer. Typical uses of buzzers and beepers include alarm devices, timers and confirmation of user input such as a mouse click or keystroke.

The buzzer or beeper is an audio signaling device, which may be mechanical, electromechanical, or piezoelectric. In electronic buzzers these vibrations are made by an oscillator circuit which drives a piezo to produce the sound. In electromechanical buzzers these oscillations are self-made through a rapid switching of an electromagnet. The best example of an electromechanical buzzer is the call bell used in offices; the horn used in automobiles is another example of an electromechanical buzzer. Figure 6.12 shows the electronic buzzer used in the circuit. The beeping sound from the buzzer using the Raspberry Pi GPIO pins.

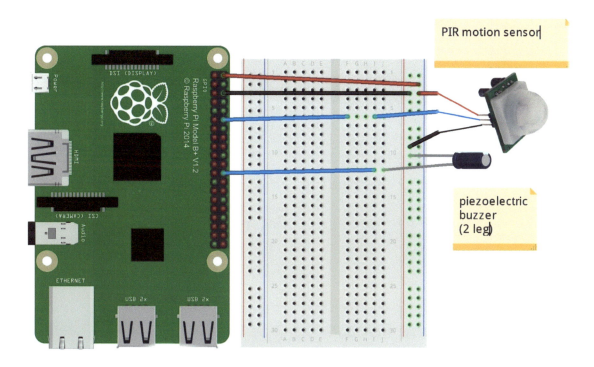

Figure 6.13: Circuit Diagram

Raspberry Pi Board	Components
2 (Vcc)	Vcc of PIR
6 (Gnd)	ground pin of PIR & short leg (-ve terminal) of Buzzer
12 (I/O pin)	Vout(Digital signal output) of PIR
24 (I/O pin)	long leg (+ve terminal) of Buzzer

Table 6.7: Circuit Connection

Program

The program for the circuit diagram shown in Figure 6.13 is given below. The connections has been summarized in the Table 6.7.

```
import RPi.GPIO as GPIO

GPIO.setmode(GPIO.BOARD)
GPIO.setwarnings(False)
```

```
GPIO.setup(26,GPIO.IN)
GPIO.setup(24,GPIO.OUT)

while True:
        insig1 = GPIO.input(26)
        print('Security Alarm 0-no movement 1-motion
        detected; Current Status : ',insig1)
        if insig1 == True:
                GPIO.output(24,True)
        else:
                GPIO.output(24,False)
```

6.6 Obstacle Avoidance Robot

An obstacle avoiding robot is an intelligent device, which can automatically sense and over-come obstacles on its path. It is developed without micro-controller in order to eliminate critical circuits, difficult programming etc. All you want to do is to just understand the circuit diagram and start doing this robot. This simple technique can be incorporated in wheeled robots to keep them away from damages and accidents.

What's required?

This intelligent robot requires several components to bring them alive. It doesn't cost too much, and easily available in all electronics markets as well.
1. **Chassis (1)**
2. **Wheels (2 or 4; Depending on the Chassis)**
3. **Castor Wheel (1)**
4. **12V/9V DC Motor (2 or 4; Depending on the number of wheels)**
5. **9V Battery & a battery snap(1)**
6. **DC Motor control board with L293D IC (1)**
7. **IR Tx-Rx module (1)**
8. **Raspberry Pi Model B/B+ Development Board (1)**
9. **Jumper wires (male-to-male - 11 nos.; male-to-female - 10 nos.)**

How to assemble?

A. Chassis

A chassis forms the basic body of robot by supporting all other components. The chassis can be made of any rigid material. Fix two DC motors to the chassis in opposite directions using nuts and bolts. Connect two wheels on the shaft of the two motors. Fix the castor wheel below the chassis at its front-end. Place the Right IR Module in top-right of lengthy cardboard, and Left IR Module in top-left of lengthy cardboard.

B. Wheel

Direction changing of the robot is acheived by halting the rotation of one of the wheels while the other wheel rotates in the opposite direction as shown in Figure 6.16.

C. Battery & Motor control board

The direction of motor rotation can be changed using the power source connected to the dc motor via the motor control board as shown in Figure 6.17.

D. Motor

Different types of motors that can be used to drive wheels are: DC motor, AC motor, Stepper motor and Servo motor. E. IR Sensor Module

Connections

The physical connections of components connected to the chassis using the connecting jumper wires has been listed in Figure 6.21. The connection from Raspberry Pi and other modules can be connected with the help of a Mini-breadboard fixed on the chassis using a double-sided sticky tape.

How does it work?

After finishing the assembling work, connect the 9V battery via battery snap. Then, see what happens. The robot will automatically start traveling on the unstructured path without hitting any objects.

When the left IR module senses any obstacles on its way, it will turn right till it stops sensing. Similarly, it will turn left when the right IR module senses obstacles. If both the sensors sense an obstacle, then the robot will move in the reverse direction and then move forward turning to its side on detecting any obstacle on the way.

Figure 6.22 shows a working model of the Obstacle Avoiding Robot with Raspberry Pi module connected to the breadboard.

Program

```
import RPi.GPIO as GPIO
```

```python
import time

#IRM1_pin = 12
#IRM2_pin = 16
GPIO.setmode(GPIO.BOARD)
GPIO.setwarnings(False)
GPIO.setup(12, GPIO.IN)
GPIO.setup(16, GPIO.IN)
GPIO.setup(18, GPIO.OUT)
GPIO.setup(22, GPIO.OUT)
GPIO.setup(11, GPIO.OUT)
GPIO.setup(13, GPIO.OUT)

def setup():
        GPIO.output(18,False)
        GPIO.output(22,False)
        GPIO.output(11,False)
        GPIO.output(13,False)


while True:

        setup()
        time.sleep(1)          # 1 second delay (1000ms)

        sig1 = GPIO.input(12)
        sig2 = GPIO.input(16)

        if sig1 == False and sig2 == False:
                print('Status sig1 sig2 :-',sig1,sig2)
                GPIO.output(18,True)
                GPIO.output(13,True)
        elif sig1 == False and sig2 == True:
                print('Status sig1 sig2 :-',sig1,sig2)
                GPIO.output(22,True)
                GPIO.output(11,True)
                time.sleep(1)     # 1 second delay (1000ms)
                GPIO.output(22,False)
```

```python
            GPIO.output(11,False)
            GPIO.output(13,True)
    elif sig1==True and sig2==False:
            print('Status sig1 sig2 :-',sig1,sig2)
            GPIO.output(22,True)
            GPIO.output(11,True)
            time.sleep(1)    # 1 second delay (1000ms)
            GPIO.output(22,False)
            GPIO.output(11,False)
            GPIO.output(18,True)
    elif sig1==True and sig2==True:
            print('Status sig1 sig2 :-',sig1,sig2)
            GPIO.output(22,True)
            GPIO.output(11,True)
            time.sleep(2)    # 2 seconds delay (2000ms)
            GPIO.output(11,False)
            time.sleep(1)    # 1 second delay (1000ms)

time.sleep(1)        # 1 second delay (1000ms)
```

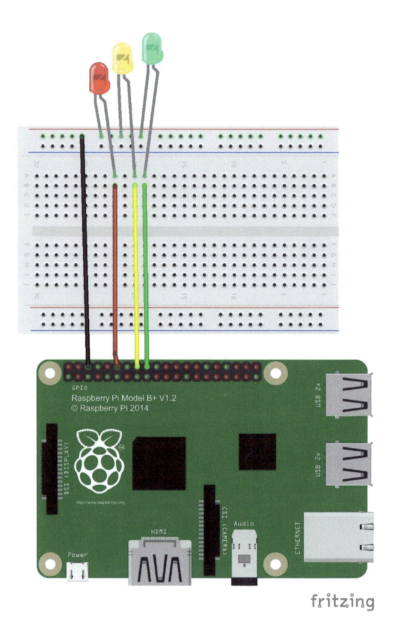

Figure 6.6: Circuit Diagram

Figure 6.7: Push-button

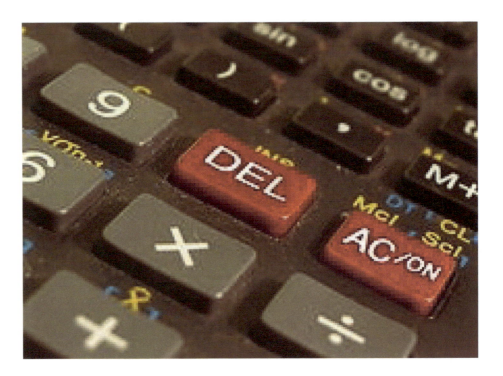

Figure 6.8: Buttons on a handheld calculator

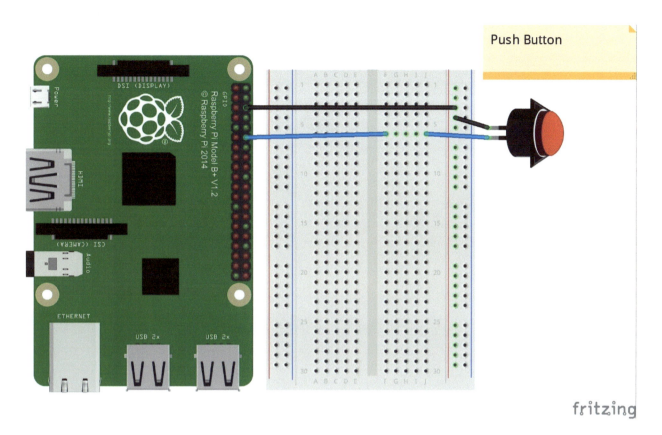

Figure 6.10: Circuit Diagram I

Figure 6.12: Buzzer

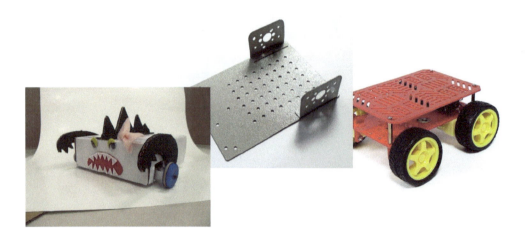

Figure 6.14: Chassis-Different Types

Figure 6.15: Different types of wheels

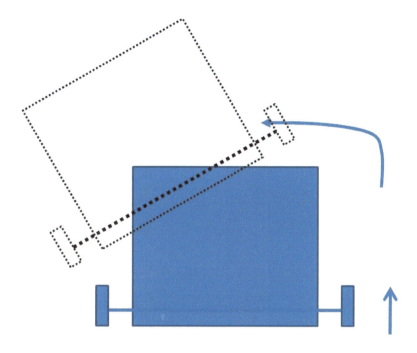

Figure 6.16: Wheel movement

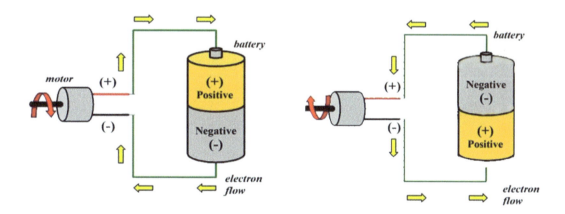

Figure 6.17: Direction of DC motor rotation using the power source (9V battery)

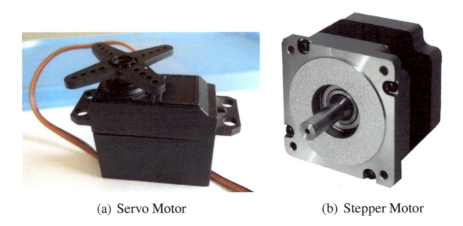

(a) Servo Motor (b) Stepper Motor

Figure 6.18: Types of Motors

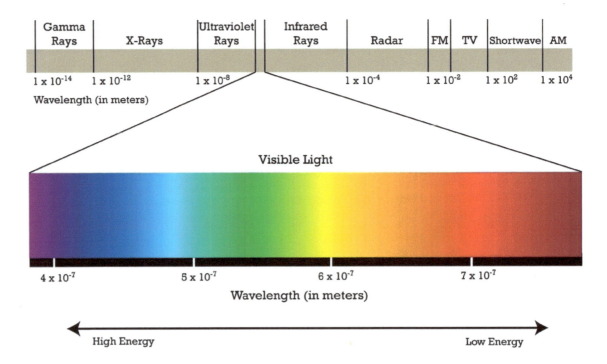

Figure 6.19: Electomagnetic Spectrum with IR

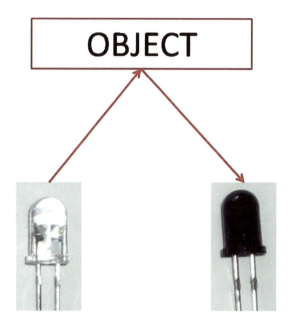

Figure 6.20: Object Detection using IR Transmitter and IR Receiver

Raspberry Pi Model B+		Other Modules	
Board Pin Numbering	BCM Pin Description	Module Name	Connections
2, 6	Supply rails 5V, GND	Common connections as required by all modules	
11	GPIO 17	Motor Driver (Right Wheel Control)	C2-B
12	GPIO 18	IR module (Right side)	OUT signal
13	GPIO 27	Motor Driver (Right Wheel Control)	C2-A
16	GPIO 23	IR module (Left side)	OUT signal
18	GPIO 24	Motor Driver (Left Wheel Control)	C1-B
22	GPIO 25	Motor Driver (Left Wheel Control)	C1-A

Figure 6.21: Connections

Figure 6.22: Obstacle Avoidance Robot

7. Safety Measures

Here we learn few important things to be kept in mind as a safety measure while doing projects in a Raspberry Pi.

1. Do not input a voltage greater that 5V to the device.
2. Always remove the power cable from the supply end.
3. Always shut down the device first before removing the power cable. The device can be shut down by entering **sudo shutdown -h** now at the terminal window. Otherwise, the memory card may get corrupt.
4. Always be careful while making connections to the GPIO pins. Care should be taken not to short the GPIO pins.
5. Do not try to run electronic devices that require a large current(DC motor, Servo motor, solenoid valve, etc.) directly using the GPIO pins. Doing this can cause damage to the device.

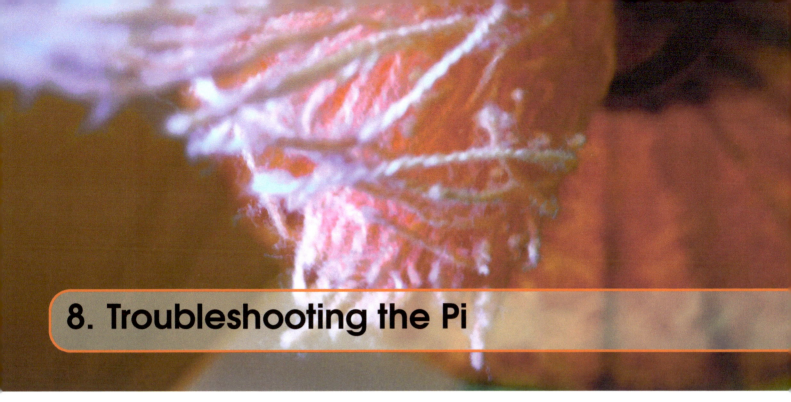

8. Troubleshooting the Pi

Five LEDs are present near the USB port which can be used to check whether the device is running normally or not. The normal behaviour of these LEDs are as follows.

LED	Colour	Function	Normal Status
ACT	Green	Card Status	Flashing during SD card activity
PWR	Red	Power	Steady ON when Pi receives some power
FDX	Orange	Full Duplex	On when Ethernet connection is full duplex
LNK	Orange	Link	On when Ethernet is connected
100	Orange	100 Mbps	On when connection is 100 Mbps off when 10 Mbps

Some of the common problems that can occur are as follows.

1. Red power LED does not light, nothing on display

This error occurs when there is a problem with the power supplied to the device. Check whether the power cable is properly connected to the device.

2. Red power LED is blinking

This error indicates that the power supplied is insufficient to power the device. This happens when the input voltage gets dropped below 4.5V. Use a different power cable to power the device if this problem arises.

3. Red power LED is on, green LED does not flash, nothing on display

This problem occurs when the device is not able to find a proper image file of the OS in the SD card. Check whether the SD card is inserted properly. If the card is inserted correctly, then it might be the problem of a corrupted SD card. In that case, install the OS image once again.

4. Green LED blinks in a specific pattern

This error also indicates a corrupted SD card. Reinstalling the OS can solve this problem.

5. Coloured splash screen

Sometimes, while booting up the device, the screen will be displayed with a coloured splash screen and it will remain in the screen. This again is a problem with the OS loaded in the SD card. This can be solved by reinstalling the OS.

After showing the splash screen, if the device gets rebooted by itself, then it indicates a problem with the power supply. This happens when the current demand of the device is not met by the power supply. If the device is powered by a USB cable connected to a computer or laptop, replace the power supply by using a micro-USB power adaptor. If you are using a micro-USB power adaptor, check the current rating of the adaptor and replace it with another one having a higher current output.

6. Kernel Panic on boot

While booting the device, some text will be shown on the screen, but the device will then hang displaying some debug messages. This error occurs when any of the USB devices connected such as mouse, keyboard, web camera, etc. are malfunctioning. Try connecting the USB devices one by one and find out the device that is malfunctioning and replace it with a properly working piece.

7. Raspberry Pi shuts down or restarts soon after booting up

This happens when the input voltage applied is too low to power the Raspberry Pi.

9. DIY Project Ideas

The Raspberry Pi can be used for implementing a wide array projects of varying applications. This can range from simple hobby projects to industrial grade products. The powerful ARM processor also enables the user to develop advanced projects consisting of real time image processing. The device can itself be used as a replacement for a computer with low computing requirements.

Some project ideas that can be easily implemented by Raspberry Pi beginners are explained in the section given below.

1. Raspberry Pi based Home Automation

You can use you Raspberry Pi module for controlling the devices in your home via the internet from a distant place. This can be done by connecting the devices in your home to a relay whose control signals are controlled by the GPIO pins of the Raspberry Pi. Then the Raspberry Pi has to configured to act as a web server. The Raspberry Pi can then be connected to the internet using the ethernet port. You can then login to the Raspberry Pi using the web address assigned by you and the devices can be controlled from anywhere in the world via internet.

2. Home security system

The Raspberry Pi module can be easily configured to function as a fully automatic home security system. A camera connected to the Raspberry Pi can be used for recording videos.

If the Raspberry Pi configures as a web server, you can even monitor your home remotely from other locations using an internet connection. The Raspberry Pi module can be even set up as a intrusion detection system using a Passive Infra Red(PIR) module. These are small IR detectors which can detect the presence of humans from their body heat. A PIR sensor can be connected to the GPIO pin as an input. If a human is detected by the device, it will send a digital high to the Raspberry Pi module which can be used for triggering an alarm or even can be programmed to capture an image or video using a web camera connected to the Raspberry Pi module.

3. Ball tracking robot

Using a web camera and minimal image processing, a robot can be developed that can track an object of particular interest. For example, a ball tracking robot can be easily made using a Raspberry Pi module and a web camera. The image captured using the web camera can be analysed to detect the presence of a round object. If an object is found, then find its centre point and send signals to the motor of the robot to make adjustments so that the centre point of the round object is aligned to the centre of the image.

4. FM radio transmitter

The Raspberry Pi module can be easily turned to an FM transmitter. Several libraries are available in the internet which can be used to set up the Raspberry Pi as an FM transmitter such as PiFM, PiFMPlay, etc. After installing the required library you can transmit an audio file through a GPIO pin attached to a 30cm long wire, which acts as the antenna of the transmitter.

5. Obstacle avoidance robot

A simple obstacle avoidance robot can be developed using a Raspberry Pi and an Infra Red(IR) obstacle sensor. IR obstacle sensors consist of a pair of IR transmitter and IR receiver. The module continuously transmit IR signals and when an obstacle present in front of the sensor, the signal will reflected back which will be received by the IR receiver which will output a signal indicating the presence of an obstacle. Using a pair of these obstacle sensors, one can easily configure a Raspberry Pi based obstacle avoidance robot.